Reading the Old Testament Through Jewish Eyes Leader Guide

Reading the Old Testament Through Jewish Eyes

Book

978-1-7910-0624-2 Paperback
978-1-7910-0625-9 ePub

Leader Guide

978-1-7910-0626-6 Paperback
978-1-7910-0627-3 ePub

DVD

978-1-7910-0628-0

Also by Rabbi Evan Moffic

What Every Christian Needs to Know About Judaism

What Every Christian Needs to Know About Passover

What Every Christian Needs to Know About the Jewishness of Jesus

First the Jews

Shalom for the Heart

LEADER GUIDE

Reading The Old Testament Through Jewish Eyes

Rabbi Evan Moffic

Leader Guide by Clara Welch

Abingdon Press | Nashville

READING THE OLD TESTAMENT THROUGH JEWISH EYES LEADER GUIDE

ISBN 978-1-7910-0626-6

21 22 23 24 25 26 27 28 29 30—10 9 8 7 6 5 4 3 2 1
MANUFACTURED IN THE UNITED STATES OF AMERICA

Contents

To the Leader

Welcome! Thank you for accepting the invitation to serve as the facilitator for this study of *Reading the Old Testament Through Jewish Eyes* by Rabbi Evan Moffic. You and your group of learners will journey together toward a greater understanding of the Torah.

This six-session study includes the following components:

- the book *Reading the Old Testament Through Jewish Eyes* by Rabbi Evan Moffic;
- this Leader Guide;
- a DVD with video segments for each of the six chapters in the book. The videos are also available to stream via a subscription to Amplify Media (www.amplifymedia.com).

It will be helpful if participants obtain a copy of the book in advance and read chapter 1 before the first session. Each participant will need a Bible. It is recommended that participants also have a notebook, journal, or electronic device for taking notes, recording insights, and noting questions during the study.

Session Format

Every group is different. These session plans have been designed to give you flexibility and choices. A variety of activities and discussion questions are included. In many cases your session time will be too short to do everything that is suggested here. As you plan each session, keep the session goals in mind and select the activities and discussion questions that will be most meaningful for your group.

Read the section titled "Before the Session" several days in advance of your meeting time as some activities suggest advance preparations.

Each session plan follows this outline.

- Planning the Session
  - ◊ Session Goals
  - ◊ Biblical Foundation
  - ◊ Before the Session
- Getting Started
  - ◊ Greetings and Introductions
  - ◊ Leading into the Story
  - ◊ Opening Prayer
- Video Study and Discussion
- Bible Study and Discussion
- Book Study and Discussion
- Optional Activity
- Wrapping Up
  - ◊ Closing Activity
  - ◊ Closing Prayer

Preparing for the Session

- Pray for the Holy Spirit to lead you as you prepare for the study. Pray for discernment for yourself and for each member of the study group.
- Before each session, familiarize yourself with the content. Read the book chapter again and watch the video segment. Read the Scripture passages that support each session. Feel free to consult different translations.
- Read through the session's plan, then go back and choose the activities and questions you wish to use during the session. Decide how much time you want to allow for each part of the session plan. Plan carefully, yet also be

prepared to adjust the session as group members interact and questions arise. Allow space for the Holy Spirit to move in and through the material, the group members, and you as facilitator.

- Secure in advance a TV and DVD player or a computer with projection.
- Prepare the space so that it will enhance the learning process. Ideally, group members should be seated around a table or in a circle so that all can see each other. Movable chairs are best so participants may easily form pairs or small groups for discussion.
- Bring a supply of Bibles for those who forget to bring their own. It is helpful to have a variety of translations.
- For each session you will also need a markerboard and markers, a chalkboard and chalk, or an easel with paper and markers.

Shaping the Learning Environment

- Begin and end on time.
- Create a climate of openness, encouraging group members to participate as they feel comfortable. Remember that some people will jump right in with answers and comments, while others will need time to process what is being discussed.
- If you notice that some group members don't enter the conversation, ask them if they have thoughts to share. Give everyone a chance to talk, but keep the conversation moving. Try to prevent a few individuals from doing all the talking.
- Communicate the importance of group discussions and group activities.
- If no one answers at first during discussions, don't be afraid of pauses. Count silently to ten; then say something such as

"Would anyone like to go first?" If no one responds, venture an answer yourself and ask for comments.

- Model openness as you share with the group. Group members will follow your example. If you limit your sharing to a surface level, others will follow suit.
- Encourage multiple answers or responses before moving on.
- Ask, "Why?" or "Why do you believe that?" or "Can you say more about that?" to help continue a discussion and give it greater depth.
- Affirm others' responses with comments such as "Great" or "Thanks" or "Good insight."
- Monitor your own contributions. If you find yourself doing most of the talking, step back so that you don't train the group to listen rather than speak up.
- Remember that you don't have all the answers. Your job is to keep the discussion going and encourage participation.

Managing the Session

- Honor the time schedule. If a session is running longer than expected, get consensus from the group before continuing beyond the agreed-upon ending time.
- Involve group members in various aspects of the group session, such as playing the DVD, saying prayers, or reading the Scripture.
- Note that the session plans sometimes call for breaking into smaller groups. This gives everyone a chance to speak and participate fully. Mix up the teams so that the same people do not pair up for every activity.
- Confidentiality is essential because some discussions and activities call for personal sharing. Let group members know that they should never pass along stories that have been shared in the group. At the beginning of each session remind

the group members that confidentiality is crucial to the success of this study.

Tips for Online Meetings

Meeting online is a great option for a number of situations. During a time of a public-health hazard, such as the COVID-19 pandemic, online meetings are a welcome opportunity for folks to converse while seeing each other's faces. Online meetings can also expand the "neighborhood" of possible group members, because people can log in from just about anywhere in the world. This also give those who do not have access to transportation or who prefer not to travel at certain times of day the chance to participate.

There are a number of platforms for online meetings. Google has two products, one called Google Hangouts and one called Google Meet. You need only a Google account to use them, and that is free.

Another popular option is Zoom. This platform is used quite a bit by businesses. If your church has an account, this can be a good medium. Individuals can obtain free accounts, but those offer meetings of no longer than forty (40) minutes. For longer meetings (which you will want for this study), you must pay for an account.

Some other platforms to consider: GoToMeeting, Web Meeting, Microsoft Teams, and others. Search the internet for "web conferencing software," and you will probably find a link to top-ten rating sites that can help you choose.

TRAINING AND PRACTICE

- Choose a platform and practice using it, so you are comfortable with it. Engage in a couple of practice runs with another person.
- Set up a training meeting.

- In advance, teach participants how to log in. Tell them that you will send them an invitation via email, and that it will include a link for them to click at the time of the meeting.
- For those who do not have internet service, let them know they may telephone into the meeting. Provide them the number and let them know that there is usually a unique phone number for each meeting.
- During the training meeting, show them the basic tools available for them to use. They can learn others as they feel more confident. Make the meeting fun by showing some amusing content, such as the Facebook page Church Humor (www.facebook.com/ChurchLOL/).

DURING THE MEETINGS

- **Early invitations.** Send out invitations at least a week in advance. Many meeting platforms enable you to do this through their software.
- **Early log in.** Participants should log in at least ten minutes in advance, to test their audio and their video connections.
- **Talking/not talking.** Instruct participants to keep their microphones muted during the meeting, so extraneous noise from their location does not interrupt the meeting. This includes chewing or yawning sounds, which can be embarrassing! When it is time for discussion, participants can unmute themselves. However, ask them to raise their hand or wave when they are ready to share, so you can call on them. Give folks a few minutes to speak up. They may not be accustomed to conversing in web conferences.

SESSION 1

THE TORAH

PLANNING THE SESSION

SESSION GOALS

- Affirm the Torah as a source of truth, wisdom, and transformation.
- Understand the difference between the terms "Torah" and "the Torah."
- Appreciate the sacred place of the Torah in Jewish life.

BIBLICAL FOUNDATION

- Deuteronomy 30:11-14

BEFORE THE SESSION

- Set up a table in the room with nametags, markers, Bibles and copies of *Reading the Old Testament Through Jewish Eyes* if these will be needed.
- Make two posters to display in the meeting space during each of the six sessions (or designate two areas of a markerboard for this purpose).

  ◊ Poster One—write these two definitions:

  1. "Torah"—teaching or process,
  2. "the Torah"—the first five books of the Bible.

◊ Poster Two—write the names of the first five books of the Bible:

- Genesis, Exodus, Leviticus, Numbers, Deuteronomy.
- You may want to list the Hebrew words you will discuss during the session on a board or piece of chart paper.

Getting Started

GREETINGS AND INTRODUCTIONS

- Greet participants as they arrive.
- Invite participants to make a nametag and pick up a Bible and/or copy of *Reading the Old Testament Through Jewish Eyes* by Rabbi Evan Moffic if they did not bring these.
- Introduce yourself and share why you are excited about facilitating this study of the book *Reading the Old Testament Through Jewish Eyes*.
- Invite participants to introduce themselves and share the name of the faith community they call home. If anyone does not currently participate in a faith community, invite them to visit your church.

HOUSEKEEPING

- Share any necessary information about your meeting space and parking.
- Let participants know you will be faithful to the time and encourage everyone to arrive on time.
- Encourage participants to read the upcoming chapter each week and do any "homework" that may be suggested.
- You may want to invite participants to bring a notebook, journal, or electronic tablet for the study. Explain that these can be used to record questions and insights, and to take notes during each session.

- Ask participants to covenant together to respect a policy of confidentiality within the group.

LEADING INTO THE STUDY

Invite participants to respond to these questions:

- What sparked your interest in participating in this group study of R*eading the Old Testament Through Jewish Eyes*? (*Let participants know it is fine if some of the reasons are repeated.*)
- What is the author's purpose for this book? (*This is stated in the first section of the chapter "The Torah."*)

Let the group know that one of the goals for each session during the study will be to affirm the Torah as a source of "truth, wisdom, and transformation" in our lives.

OPENING PRAYER

Loving God, thank you for the Bible. Thank you for the early historians, storytellers, and scribes who kept these ancient words alive, who preserved them on scrolls, and who passed them down through the generations. Open our hearts and minds to receive your love and your teachings that are revealed in these sacred writings; In the name of your Son Jesus Christ we pray. Amen.

Video Study and Discussion

Invite participants to consider these questions as they view the video:

- What is one thing you learned that you did not know before?
- Rabbi Moffic describes the special care that scribes take when preparing a Torah scroll. What does this say about

the Jewish appreciation for the Torah? What do Christians approach with similar care?
- Rabbi Moffic shares that the Torah is a book for all people, of all faiths. What can Jews and Christians learn from one another as we study the Torah?
- What do you hope to gain from participating in this study?

Following the video, invite volunteers to share their responses to the questions above.

Bible Study and Discussion

Ask a volunteer to read Deuteronomy 6:5-7 aloud.

Point out that the commandment to love is at the heart of God's instructions in the Torah.

Highlight Rabbi Moffic's point that God speaks to everyone, not just the Jews, through the Torah.

Say:

- As I read Deuteronomy 30:11-14 listen for the one word or phrase that catches your attention.

Read the passage aloud:

> *Surely, this Instruction which I enjoin upon you this day is not too baffling for you, nor is it beyond reach. It is not in the heavens, that you should say, "Who among us can go up to the heavens and get it for us and impart it to us, that we may observe it?" Neither is it beyond the sea, that you should say, "Who among us can cross to the other side of the sea and get it for us and impart it to us, that we may observe it?" No, the thing is very close to you, in your mouth and in your heart, to observe it (Deuteronomy 30:11-14).*

Ask:

- What is the word or phrase that caught your attention? (*You may want to list these on a board or piece of chart paper.*)

Say:

- As I read this passage of Scripture a second time, reflect on what God might be saying to you through this word or phrase.

After you read the Scripture passage a second time ask:

- What do you hear God saying to you through this Scripture?

BOOK STUDY AND DISCUSSION

WHAT IS TORAH?

Explain the difference in the meaning of "Torah" and "the Torah."

- Used alone, the word "Torah" means teaching or process. The study of "Torah" includes the study of all sacred Jewish texts.
- The phrase "the Torah" always means the first five books of the Bible.

Explain that this study will focus on "the Torah."

Invite participants to refer to the section titled "What is Torah?" as they respond to these questions. Ask:

- What does the Hebrew word *parashiyot* mean? (*"Torah portions" or sections—there are fifty-four* parashiyot *in the Torah. One "Torah Portion" is read in the synagogue every week.*)
- Who reads the Torah in the synagogue each week?
- What does the Hebrew word *nusach* mean? (*melody for chanting the Hebrew text*)

- Why is the *nusach* important?
- What melodies, songs, and hymns help you remember verses of Scripture?

LETTERS IN THE TORAH

This section of the chapter contains a large number of details about the writing and reading of the Torah scroll. Call attention to these main points. The Torah scroll:

- is written in a sacred style;
- is handled with careful attention;
- rests in a special place when it is not being read;
- is read to the congregation with ways to ensure accuracy.

Review the meaning of these Hebrew words:

- *sofer* means both "scribe" and "to count." The scribes use a special ink and a special writing quill and traditionally count the letters on the Torah scroll;
- *yad* literally means hand. A "yad" is a pointer used by the reader of the Torah scroll to avoid touching the scroll. The oils and bacteria on a person's skin may cause the parchment to erode;
- The receptacle or "ark" in which the Torah scroll rests in the synagogue is known by three names:
  - ◊ *aron hakodesh*—the holy ark;
  - ◊ *teva*—the same Hebrew word used in reference to Noah's ark—Noah's ark and the Torah both sustain life;
  - ◊ *heikhal*—palace—holy inner sanctum of the sanctuary in the Jerusalem Temple.

Invite participants to refer to the section "Letters in the Torah" as they respond to these questions. Ask:

- Why do the scribes believe it is important to count each letter of a Torah scroll?

- Why is no metal used in the creation of a Torah scroll?
- What is meant by the statement, "God is in the details"?
- In what ways does the Torah represent "God on earth" for the Jewish community?

Blessings and Prayers

Explain that the Torah is read aloud in Hebrew. While many in the congregation will be able to understand Hebrew, most will not be fluent. In many synagogues the worshippers are provided with a printed commentary that contains both the Hebrew and the English texts for the Torah portion that is read aloud.

Call attention to these Hebrew words and definitions:

- *baal korei*—Torah reader who chants the Torah portion;
- *gabbai*—a person who stands with the Torah reader to correct any mistakes that will change the meaning of the text;
- *nikudot* —vowels, not included in Hebrew scrolls, which means a word may be read incorrectly and change the meaning of the text;
- *aliyah* (singular), *aliyot* (plural)—blessings over the Torah, offered by someone other than the Torah reader both before and after the Torah portion is chanted;
- *hagba*—ritual of lifting the Torah scroll after the reading.

Explain that the literal translation of the Hebrew word "*aliyah*" (blessing over the Torah) is "ascent." Ask:

- In what ways does the word *ascent* describe the Jewish community's experience with the Torah? (*See section titled "How Torah Is Read."*)
- In what ways does the word *ascent* describe the experience of Christians with the Bible?

Note Rabbi Moffic's observation that communal prayers are offered before the Torah is returned to the ark because "Somehow God feels more present while the Torah is out."

Optional Activity

Summarize the information presented in the section "Other Practices" about the three primary denominations in modern Judaism.

Highlight the author's comment:

> The Torah has sustained the Jewish people for thousands of years because it speaks to and guides us in our deepest human needs and possibilities.

Ask:

- In what ways does the Bible, including the Torah, sustain you?

Wrapping Up

CLOSING ACTIVITY

Read or summarize the last several paragraphs of the section titled *Hagba* about the prayers the congregation recites as the Torah is returned to the ark.

Invite participants to share thoughts and ideas related to the Hebrew word *teshuvah* and the acts of "repentance" and "return."

Encourage participants to review the closing section of the chapter titled "Structure" for an overview of the first five books of the Bible.

CLOSING PRAYER

Loving God, thank you for the Torah. Guide us as we study these ancient writings. Help us to listen carefully so that we may hear what you are saying to us today through these holy words. Amen.

SESSION 2

GENESIS

PLANNING THE SESSION

SESSION GOALS

- Affirm the Torah as a source of truth, wisdom, and transformation.
- Consider the similarities between family life in ancient times and today.
- Discover what Genesis teaches about our relationship with God and with each other.

BIBLICAL FOUNDATION

- Genesis 1:27; 2:7; 2:21-23

BEFORE THE SESSION

- Set up a table in the room with nametags, markers, Bibles, and copies of *Reading the Old Testament Through Jewish Eyes* if these will be needed.
- Display the two posters from session 1:
  ◊ Poster One—definitions of "Torah" and "The Torah"
  ◊ Poster Two—Genesis, Exodus, Leviticus, Numbers, Deuteronomy.

- In preparation for "Leading into the Study," draw a vertical line down the middle of a board or piece of chart paper to make two columns. Write the heading "Beautiful" in the first column and "Messy" in the second column.

GETTING STARTED

GREETINGS AND INTRODUCTIONS

- Greet participants as they arrive.
- If there are newcomers allow time for introductions.
- Review information from "Housekeeping" in session 1, including the covenant to respect confidentiality within the group.

LEADING INTO THE STUDY

Call attention to these key points in the introduction to this chapter:

- Much of Genesis centers on a single family, their relationship with God, and their relationships with one another.
- In ancient times and in the present day, individuals within families experience conflict with one another.

During the discussion of the questions below write responses under the headings "Beautiful" and "Messy." Ask:

- What are beautiful aspects of family life today?
- What are messy aspects of family life today?

Remind the group that one of the goals for this study is to grow in our understanding of the Torah as a source of "truth, wisdom, and transformation."

OPENING PRAYER

Loving God, thank you for the gift of the Torah. Open our eyes to the wisdom revealed in these ancient writings. Help us put these lessons into practice in our relationships with our families and friends; in the name of your Son Jesus Christ we pray. Amen.

VIDEO STUDY AND DISCUSSION

Invite participants to consider these questions as they view the video:

- Rabbi Moffic describes the orderliness of creation, which we see in the first creation account. Where do you see order in the created world as you look around?
- How does the idea of "the image of God" stand at the heart of ethics and moral values in the Torah?
- What movement does Rabbi Moffic identify from the beginning to the end of Genesis? How do we see this play out among the families whose story Genesis tells?
- What is something you discovered that you did not know before?

Following the video, invite volunteers to share their responses to the questions above.

BIBLE STUDY AND DISCUSSION

Invite a volunteer to read Genesis 1:27 aloud:

> *And God created man in His image, in the image of God He created him; male and female He created them.*

Ask:

- How would you summarize the main idea of this verse?

- What are examples of human inequality present today?
- How does Genesis 1:27 call us to affirm equality among all human beings?

Read Genesis 2:7:

> *The* LORD *God formed man from the dust of the earth. He blew into his nostrils the breath of life, and man became a living being.*

Ask:

- How does Genesis 2:7 affirm our close relationship with our Creator? (*God fashioned us with God's own hands and gave us life with God's own breath.*)

Read Genesis 2:22-23.

> *And the* LORD *God fashioned the rib that He had taken from the man into a woman; and He brought her to the man. Then the man said, "This one at last Is bone of my bones and flesh of my flesh. This one shall be called Woman, For from man was she taken."*

Ask:

- What is the significance of the words *ish* and *ishah* in Genesis 2:22-23? (*Note Rabbi Moffic's point that our unique personalities emerge as we live in relationship with other people.*)
- Taken together, what do these three Scripture passages from Genesis tell us about our relationship with God and with each other?

Book Study and Discussion

CAIN AND ABEL

Read the story of Cain and Abel in Genesis 4:1-16.

Explain that this story does not indicate why God preferred one sacrifice over the other, and that later the Torah allows offerings of produce as well as livestock.

Read again verses 5b and 6. Ask:

- What are the key points in these verses? (*God was present for Cain and promised to accept him; God offered Cain a choice about how to respond to his anger.)*

Read again Genesis 4:8. Note that the original text has a gap and does not say what Cain said to Abel. Ask:

- If this gap is intentional, what does this say about the way Cain handled his anger?
- What offers of help and support did Cain ignore?
- How do you react/respond when you feel angry toward a family member or a close friend?
- How well do you communicate your feelings of rejection, hurt, and anger to the others involved?
- How well do you listen when others share their feelings with you?
- What can we learn from this story?

ABRAHAM

Read Genesis 12:1-3, God's call to Abraham. If time permits begin with Genesis 11:27 and read through to Genesis 12:9.

Highlight Rabbi Moffic's observation that Abraham's journey is about more than traveling to another land. It is also about "self-discovery, differentiation, and maturity."

Ask:

- What key steps does Rabbi Moffic identify in this journey of self-discovery?
- How have you experienced these steps in your life's journey?
- In what ways is Abraham's story similar to your story?

JACOB AND ESAU

Call attention to two purposes in the story of Jacob and Esau:

- Theological—to show that God chose Jacob to carry on the covenant God made with Abraham and Isaac;
- Relational—to provide lessons about human relationships.

Read or summarize the story of Jacob and Esau recorded in Genesis:

- Birth (25:19-26)
- Esau gives up his birthright (25:27-34)
- Esau marries (26:34-35)
- Isaac blesses Jacob (27:1-29)
- Esau responds to Jacob's deceit (27:30-41)

Ask:

- What does the biblical text tell us about:
  - ◊ Esau?
  - ◊ Jacob?
  - ◊ Isaac?
  - ◊ Rebekah?

Read the account of Esau's forgiveness and the reconciliation between brothers in Genesis 33:1-17.

Ask:

- How might the passage of time lead to the healing of conflicts?
- In contrast, how might the passage of time solidify conflicts and make reconciliation difficult?
- What helped Jacob be open to accepting forgiveness and reconciliation?
- Why was Esau able to forgive Jacob and offer reconciliation?

JOSEPH AND HIS FATHER

Read Genesis 37:9-14.

Invite participants to refer to the section "Joseph and His Father" as they respond to these questions. Ask:

- Why was Jacob angry about Joseph's dream?
- Why did Joseph not reach out to his father after he rose to power in Egypt?
- How did this misunderstanding between father and son hurt Jacob? (Genesis 37:31-35)
- How did it hurt Joseph?
- How do misunderstandings and misinterpretations of events hurt relationships within families and among friends today?

OPTIONAL ACTIVITY

Offer time for silent reflection and journaling.

Suggest that participants reflect on these questions during this time:

- What have I learned from the Book of Genesis about relationships?
- Who do I need to forgive?
- From whom do I need to seek forgiveness?
- With whom do I hope to experience reconciliation?

Wrapping Up

CLOSING ACTIVITY

Read or summarize the closing section titled "Reconciliation."

CLOSING PRAYER

Loving God, thank you for the Torah. Guide us as we study these ancient writings. Help us to listen carefully so that we may hear what you are saying to us today through these holy words. Amen.

Session 3

Exodus

Planning the Session

SESSION GOALS

- Affirm the Torah as a source of truth, wisdom, and transformation.
- Discern how experiences in our past strengthen us to respond to God's call in the present.
- Examine the experiences that led Moses to be God's spokesperson and leader for the Israelites.

BIBLICAL FOUNDATION

- Exodus 1:1-8

BEFORE THE SESSION

- Set up a table in the room with nametags and markers, Bibles, and extra copies of *Reading the Old Testament Through Jewish Eyes* if these are still needed;
- Have pencils and strips of paper available, one for each person in your group.

Getting Started

GREETINGS AND INTRODUCTIONS

- Greet participants as they arrive.
- If there are newcomers, allow time for introductions.
- Review information from "Housekeeping" in session 1, including the covenant to respect confidentiality within the group.

LEADING INTO THE STUDY

- Distribute paper and pencils.
- Instruct participants to write a one-sentence introduction beginning with "I am (name)" followed by one statement about himself or herself.
- Invite volunteers to share their one-sentence introductions.
- Say: Listen to the way God introduced Godself to the Israelites: "I the LORD am your God who brought you out of the land of Egypt, the house of bondage" (Exodus 20:2).

Remind the group that one of the goals for this study is to understand the ways the Torah is a source of "truth, wisdom, and transformation" in our lives.

OPENING PRAYER

Loving God, thank you that you know our names and that you hear us when we cry out to you. Thank you for bringing us out of places of bondage and oppression and for being with us through times of fear, grief, and confusion. Help us to be mindful of others who experience various forms of slavery and oppression. Let us speak and act in your name to help bring freedom to others; in the name of your Son Jesus Christ we pray. Amen.

Video Study and Discussion

Invite participants to consider these questions as they view the video:

- The ancient Egyptians were powerful, yet it was their slaves, the Israelites, who survived and thrived because of God's presence. What does God's favor of the Israelites say about God's character?
- What is the role of laws for God's people? Why are laws important, and how does observing them bring us closer to God?
- How does working together shape us as a people of faith? When has cooperation and a shared responsibility drawn you closer to other members of your faith community?
- What is one thing you learned from the video that you did not know before?

Following the video, invite volunteers to share their responses to the questions above.

Bible Study and Discussion

Explain that the Hebrew title for the Book of Exodus is *Shemot,* which means "Names."

Read Exodus 1:1-7.

> *These are the names of the sons of Israel who came to Egypt with Jacob, each coming with his household: Reuben, Simeon, Levi, and Judah; Issachar, Zebulun, and Benjamin; Dan and Naphtali, Gad and Asher. The total number of persons that were of Jacob's issue came to seventy, Joseph being already in Egypt. Joseph died, and all his brothers, and all that generation. But the Israelites were fertile and prolific; they multiplied and increased very greatly, so that the land was filled with them.*

Ask:

- Why are these names important? (*Recall that Jacob and his twelve sons are the descendants of Abraham and Isaac, whom God promised to make into a great nation [see Genesis 12:2].*)

Read Exodus 1:8.

> *A new king arose over Egypt who did not know Joseph.*

Ask:

- Why is it significant that the new king (or new pharaoh) did not know Joseph?
- What names do you believe it is important for us to remember and why? (*Responses may include names of well-known people from history and names of family members and friends.*)

Book Study and Discussion

SLAVERY AND EXODUS

Call attention to Rabbi Moffic's point that the Israelites' experience of slavery in Egypt was both their darkest hour to date and a significant turning point in their life as a nation.

If you sense that participants in your group are not familiar with the biblical account of Israel's experience of slavery in Egypt, be prepared to read or summarize Exodus 1:8-22 and 2:23-25.

Note Rabbi Moffic's key points about the Israelites' experience of slavery and the Exodus:

- It is the context for the birth of the Jewish people.

- It is a strong example of how a shared experience of adversity creates solidarity among a people.
- It informs the Jewish people's understanding of God who identifies himself as "I the LORD am your God who brought you out of the land of Egypt, the house of bondage" (Exodus 20:2).
- It establishes our core belief that God is on the side of people who experience oppression and injustice;
- It is the context for the commandment, "You shall not wrong a stranger or oppress him, for you were strangers in the land of Egypt" (Exodus 22:20).

Ask:

- What events in the Bible provide the foundation for our Christian emphasis on justice?

MOSES—FIRST EXPERIENCE

Using the section "Three Experiences of Moses" as a guide:

- Review the story of the birth and childhood of Moses;
- Note that the Torah introduces Moses as an adult by first describing three times when he acted on behalf of victims of injustice;
- Read the account of these experiences recorded in Exodus 2:11-17.

Ask:

- What insights from the Jewish sages and theologians add meaning to the interpretation of Moses's actions on behalf of justice?

Note Rabbi Moffic's observation that God gave Moses "a passion for justice" and then put Moses in places where his passion for justice was needed. Ask:

- What passion(s) for service and ministry has God given you?
- When have you been in a place where your particular passion(s) for service and ministry were needed?

MOSES—SECOND EXPERIENCE

Note that there are a number of interpretations in Jewish and Christian theology related to the story of Moses and the burning bush. The interpretation presented in this chapter may be unfamiliar to Christians.

Read Exodus 3:1-12. Share these key points:

- Moses is now married and living a peaceful life as a shepherd;
- The story of Moses and the burning bush continues in Exodus 3:13–4:17;
- Moses could have walked away at any time.

Ask:

- What do the Jewish sages teach about why Moses stayed and conversed with God? (*Moses heard the voice as that of his father.*)

Call attention to Rabbi Moffic's present-day story and ask:

- When have you heard the voice of a parent or other significant person that helped you decide what to do?

Read Exodus 3:13-14. Call attention to the two translations for God's name.

- Present tense – "I Am Who I Am"
- Future tense – "I Will Be Who I Will Be"

Review the information in the section "I Am YHVH." Ask:

- How do the translations "I Am Who I Am" and "I Will Be Who I Will Be" enhance your understanding of who God is?

MOSES—THIRD EXPERIENCE

Read Exodus 19:1-8. Call attention to three key points about this experience at Mount Sinai:

- The people experienced unity in their collective experience of *yeirah*, Hebrew for wonder, fear, and awe.
- The Jewish sages suggest that the unity the Israelites experienced in that moment of God's revelation transcended time and space and was felt by all Jews, including future generations.
- God established "a baseline of equality" among the Jewish community.

Ask:

- What aspects of this experience of revelation at Mount Sinai stand out for you?
- When have you experienced a revelation of God?
- What was that experience like for you?

TABERNACLE

Read Exodus 25:1-2.

Note that instructions for building the Tabernacle and making clothing for the priests are found in Exodus 25–28.

You may want to allow a few minutes for participants to skim these chapters to get an idea of what was involved in building the Tabernacle. Invite participants to read verses that stand out for them.

Ask:

- How did the group project of building the Tabernacle benefit the Israelites?

Optional Activity

Invite discussion of this question:

- When have you grown in faith during a time of darkness and trial?

Share this quote by Rabbi Moffic:

> "We all have a past that preceded our birth."

Invite discussion of this question:

- What aspects of the past that preceded your birth have had a significant impact on your life?

Wrapping Up

CLOSING ACTIVITY

Remind the group that Exodus begins with the people of Israel feeling separated from God while living in bondage in Egypt.

Read Exodus 40:33-38. Ask:

- What is the situation of the Israelites at the end of the Book of Exodus?

CLOSING PRAYER

Loving God, thank you for the Torah. Guide us as we study these ancient writings. Help us to listen carefully so that we may hear what you are saying to us today through these holy words. Amen.

SESSION 4

LEVITICUS

PLANNING THE SESSION

SESSION GOALS

- Affirm the Torah as a source of truth, wisdom, and transformation.
- Understand the role of the priests in the life of the people of Israel.
- Explore how worship rituals draw us closer to God.

BIBLICAL FOUNDATION

- Luke16:10

BEFORE THE SESSION

- Set up a table in the room with nametags and markers, Bibles, and extra copies of *Reading the Old Testament Through Jewish Eyes* if these are still needed;
- Write the five Scripture passages from Leviticus 4 that will be read by volunteers (see "Sin Offering" section in this session) on separate pieces of paper. Distribute the papers to the readers as they arrive.

Getting Started

GREETINGS AND INTRODUCTIONS

- Greet participants as they arrive.
- If there are newcomers, allow time for introductions.
- Review information from "Housekeeping" in session 1, including the importance of confidentiality with the group.

LEADING INTO THE STUDY

Ask:

- What is a ritual? (*from Merriam-Webster's Dictionary: "the established form for a ceremony" specifically "the order of words prescribed for a religious ceremony"; synonyms include custom, habit, and practice.* ["Ritual." *Merriam-Webster.com Dictionary*, https://www.merriam-webster.com/dictionary/ritual. Accessed 1 June, 2021.]).
- What rituals do you observe in your church/faith community? (*Responses may include Holy Communion, baptism, weddings, funerals, passing the attendance pad or offering plate during a worship service*);
- What rituals or ceremonies do we observe in our community? (*Responses may include graduations and observances of special days*);
- What customs, practices, and observances have become rituals for you as an individual and/or for your family? (*Responses may include saying a prayer before meals, holiday traditions, and celebrations of special events*);
- In what ways do these rituals add meaning to your life?
- Which of these rituals have the power to make you more mindful of God's presence?

Remind the group that one of the goals for this study is to come to know the Torah as a source of "truth, wisdom, and transformation."

OPENING PRAYER

Loving and Holy God, thank you for calling us to live in a close relationship with you. Thank you for the rituals that remind us of your faithful presence and your never-ending love; in the name of your Son Jesus Christ we pray. Amen.

VIDEO STUDY AND DISCUSSION

Invite participants to consider these questions as they view the video:

- What does Leviticus have to teach us about the power of ritual?
- What rituals give meaning to your life and faith? What would you lose if these rituals stopped or lost their integrity?
- How do boundaries—between the sacred and the mundane—enable us to feel close to God? Why is it important to have holy spaces and times where we feel God more acutely than at other times and places?
- What is one thing you learned about Leviticus that you did not know before?

Following the video, invite volunteers to share their responses to the questions above.

BIBLE STUDY AND DISCUSSION

Read Luke16:10 prefacing the verse with "Jesus said:"

> *"Whoever is faithful with little is also faithful with much, and the one who is dishonest with little is also dishonest with much" (CEB).*

Ask:

- What is Jesus teaching us in this verse?
- How have you experienced this teaching in your life?

Note that:

- Leviticus includes detailed instructions about how to carry out the rituals;
- Rabbi Moffic observes that when we are careful about the ways we observe and participate in rituals, we will also be careful about other aspects of our lives.

Book Study and Discussion

Remind the group of God's revelation to the people of Israel at Mount Sinai recorded in Exodus 19:1-8 (see session on Exodus). God proclaimed, "You shall be to Me a kingdom of priests and a holy nation" (Exodus 19:6).

Share these key points:

- A theme in Leviticus is how Israel will live up to the call in Exodus 19:6.
- Leviticus focuses on the priests and their service in the Tabernacle and Temple.
- The priests are from the tribe of Levi, descendants of Jacob's third son.
- The priests were called to set an example and lead all Israel to holiness.
- The Book of Leviticus has two sections. Chapters 1–16 are about sacrifices and role of the priests. Chapters 17–27 are

about the Holiness Code and include instructions on how to live a holy life.

- Leviticus provides detailed descriptions of the rituals that draw the people into a holy relationship with God.

SIN OFFERING—LEVITICUS 4

To get a flavor for Leviticus 4, invite volunteers to read the following verses: Leviticus 4:1-2; 4:3; 4:13-14; 4:22-23; 4:27-28.

Ask:

- What is the purpose of the sin offering? (*to make amends for unintentional sin and restore order*)
- What do these Hebrew words mean?
  - ◊ *Shalom* (peace)
  - ◊ *Seder* (order)
  - ◊ *Chet* (sin, missing the mark)

Create small groups of two to five people. Instruct the groups to refer to the section "Sin Offering" as they consider responses to these questions:

- Why is a ritual more effective than an apology?
- Why were the details in the rituals for sin offerings important to the Israelites?

After the groups have had time to work, invite each group to share their findings.

PRIESTS—LEVITICUS 8

Read Leviticus 8:1-5. Explain that the remaining verses of Leviticus 8 describe the ritual for ordination of the priests.

Again, invite participants to work in small groups of two to five people. Instruct the groups to refer to the section "Priests" as they consider this question:

- What stands out for you in this section related to the themes of "new creation" and "sacrifice"?

After the groups have had time to work, invite each group to share their findings.

NADAB AND ABIHU—LEVITICUS 10:1-7

Read Leviticus 10:1-7. Share this background information:

- Aaron and his sons were leading the Israelites in the rituals for offering sacrifices.
- Since Mishael and Elzaphan were not priests, they were permitted to leave the sanctuary with the bodies.
- Aaron and his remaining sons were required to remain in the sanctuary to finish the sacrifices. They were wearing holy priest's clothing that could not be ripped as was customary during mourning.
- Jewish sages and theologians offer different interpretations of this incident.

Ask:

- What do you think this incident teaches about holiness?

ATONEMENT—LEVITICUS 16

In the sections "Yom Kippur" and "Grace and Forgiveness," Rabbi Moffic writes about the importance of atonement and reconciliation. Share these key points:

- *Atonement* means "at-one-ment"—making one.
- Sacrifices and rituals described in Leviticus provided a means for the Israelites to repent of their sins, accept God's forgiveness, and restore their close relationship with God.

- Yom Kippur—the Day of Atonement or Reconciliation—was celebrated once a year to cover the sins of the nation.

Ask:

- Why is reconciliation important:
  ◊ within our faith community?
  ◊ in our personal relationship with God?
  ◊ in our nation?
- What rituals provide us with a means of reconciliation? (*Responses may include the Service of Holy Communion, which includes a prayer of Confession and Pardon; the Lord's Prayer; personal prayers; World Communion Sunday; World Day of Prayer.*)

See "Optional Activity" for suggestions for delving deeper into interpretations of Leviticus 16.

LOVE YOUR NEIGHBOR AS YOURSELF—LEVITICUS 19

Share these key points:

- In Leviticus, God gives instructions to the priests about building "a culture of holiness" within the Israelite community (see the section, "Sin Offering").
- Leviticus 19 is one of the chapters in the "Holiness Code," which contains instructions for living holy lives.
- The Golden Rule, "Love your neighbor as yourself," is included in the Holiness Code (Leviticus 19:18 CEB).

Recruit four volunteers to read Leviticus 19 as follows:

- Verses 1-10;
- Verses 11-18;

- Verses 19-25,
- Verses 26-37.

Before the volunteers read these verses, invite participants to listen and make a note of any instructions that catch their attention. After the verses are read, ask:

- Which instructions caught your attention and why?
- Which instructions will help us build a culture of holiness in our present-day context?
- What does Jesus teach us about what it means for us to love our neighbor?

Optional Activity

Recruit volunteers to share the reading of Leviticus 16.

After the reading, instruct participants to refer to the sections "Yom Kippur" and "Grace and Forgiveness" as they respond to the questions below.

If you have a large group, create three small groups and assign each group one question. Then offer time for groups to share their findings.

Ask:

- What are the different interpretations of the two goats and Azazel?
- According to the Torah, what are the requirements and steps for the nation of Israel to receive reconciliation with God?
- What can we learn from this ritual of reconciliation that will help us today?

WRAPPING UP

CLOSING ACTIVITY

Invite a volunteer to read the conclusion to this chapter. Ask:

- How does Rabbi Moffic's statement that "Faith is something we do" resonate with your life?
- Who creates sacred spaces for God in our world today?
- Where are sacred spaces for you?
- In what ways is the Torah a guide for us today as Christians as we create sacred space on earth for God?

CLOSING PRAYER

Loving God, thank you for the Torah. Guide us as we study these ancient writings. Help us to listen carefully so that we may hear what you are saying to us today through these holy words. Amen.

Session 5

Numbers

Planning the Session

SESSION GOALS

- Affirm the Torah as a source of truth, wisdom, and transformation.
- Embrace God's blessing(s) in our lives.
- Recognize the importance of honesty and faith in our relationship with God.

BIBLICAL FOUNDATION

- Numbers 6:24-26

BEFORE THE SESSION

- Set up a table in the room with nametags and markers, Bibles, and extra copies of *Reading the Old Testament Through Jewish Eyes* if these are still needed;
- In preparation for "Leading into the Study," write the word *Numbers* at the top of a markerboard or large piece of paper. Then write two or three numbers that are important to you on the board or chart paper, in random fashion, not as a list. The numbers may be dates, a graduation class year, or a house number, for example.

- Decide if you want to do the "Optional Activity." If so, you may need to bring in three-by-five cards for the participants.

Getting Started

GREETINGS AND INTRODUCTIONS

- Greet participants as they arrive.
- If there are newcomers, allow time for introductions.
- Review information from "Housekeeping" in session 1, including the importance of confidentiality within the group.

LEADING INTO THE STUDY

Instruct participants to call out responses to the question below without giving any explanations. Recruit a person to serve as scribe to write the responses on the board or chart paper with the heading "Numbers." Ask:

- What numbers are important to you? (*Examples may include dates of special events, graduation class years, number of family members, years of sobriety, ages, and house numbers.*)

Then share these key points:

- The fourth book of the Torah was given the English name "Numbers" because it records several censuses of the Israelites during the wilderness journey.
- The Torah affirms that each person counts and is unique: "And God created man in His image, in the image of God He created him; male and female He created them" (Genesis 1:27).
- The Torah affirms the importance of relationships with others: "The Lord God said, "It is not good for man to be alone; I will make a fitting helper for him" (Genesis 2:18).

Instruct participants to have in mind the numbers they have just mentioned as they respond to these questions. Ask:

- How do these numbers affirm your uniqueness as a child of God?
- How do these numbers affirm the importance of your relationships with others?

Remind the group that one of the goals for this study is to grow in our understanding of the Torah as a source of "truth, wisdom, and transformation."

OPENING PRAYER

Loving God, thank you for the numbers in our lives that remind us of the people we love and the people who love us. Help us remember that you love each one of us as your beloved child, just the way we are. Open our hearts as we reach out and care for the ones you place in our lives; in the name of your Son Jesus Christ we pray. Amen.

VIDEO STUDY AND DISCUSSION

Invite participants to consider these questions as they view the video:

- Rabbi Moffic describes high and low points in the Israelites' journey in the wilderness. What do you identify as high points and low points in your faith journey?
- Rabbi Moffic says that much of faith is simply doing the same things over and over again. What repetitive, habitual actions characterize your faith? What value do you see in these acts?
- In your life, have you been shaped more by the singular, dramatic experiences, or by the everyday things that happen so often you stop noticing them?

- What is one thing you learned from the video that you did not know before?

Following the video, invite volunteers to share their responses to the questions above.

Bible Study and Discussion

Note that Numbers 6:24-26 text is a Priestly Blessing and the oldest blessing known in Judaism.

Read the blessing printed below.

> *The Lord bless you and protect you!*
> *The Lord deal kindly and graciously with you!*
> *The Lord bestow His favor upon you and grant you peace!*

Suggest that participants refer to the section "Priestly Blessing" as they respond to these questions. Ask:

- How does the text emphasize that God is the source of our blessings?
- In what ways are the priests and all people "conduits" of God's blessings?
- With what does God bless us? (*Jewish sages suggest the blessings are appropriate for each individual.*)
- Verse 24 reads, "The Lord bless you and protect you." Why might we need protection with our blessings?
- For the second line of the blessing, how does Rabbi Moffic's alternate translation, "May the light of God's face shine out from your face," enhance your understanding of the text?

You may want to close the "Bible Study and Discussion" by playing a recording of this blessing. There is a beautiful arrangement by John Rutter.

Book Study and Discussion

MOSES'S DESPAIR

Remind the group that the Hebrew name for a book in the Bible is the first significant word in that book (first paragraph in the chapter about Exodus). The Hebrew name for Numbers is *bamidbar,* which means "in the wilderness." The first phrase of Numbers says, "The Lord spoke to Moses in the wilderness of Sinai" (Numbers 1:1).

Invite a volunteer to read the results of the first census Moses and the Israelites took in the wilderness, recorded in Numbers 1:44-47. Ask:

- What do you think it was like to journey in the wilderness with so many people?

Call attention to the fact that Moses cried out to God in despair over the frustrations and failures he felt as the leader of the Israelites in the wilderness.

Read Numbers 11:11-15 as printed in the book or from a Bible. Ask:

- What questions and concerns does Moses bring to God?

Highlight Rabbi Moffic's reference to the Christian concept of "the Dark Night of the Soul" from the writings of the sixteenth-century monk St. John of the Cross. Note that an experience of "the Dark Night of the Soul" may grow out of feelings of doubt, pain, failure, darkness, and despair.

Invite participants to refer to the section "Moses's Despair" as they respond to the following questions. Ask:

- How did Moses's cry of despair and God's response transform the wilderness journey for the Israelites?

- How did Moses's cry and God's response transform Moses as a leader?
- Why is humility an important characteristic of a faithful leader for God? (*Humility involves thinking more about God and other people and less about oneself, trusting God's promises, and accepting God's call with faith.)*

The following questions are more personal in nature. Choose the option that will work best for your group:

- full group discussion;
- discussion in small groups of two to four persons;
- a few minutes of quiet time for personal reflection and journaling.

Introduce the questions by reminding the group that the word "wilderness" may be used to describe a time we felt lost, alone, fearful, and/or in despair. Ask:

- When have you felt you were journeying through a *wilderness*?
- During this time did you cry out to God? Why or why not?
- If yes, how did God respond?
- What impact did this experience have on your faith?

Rabbi Moffic writes that a journey through a wilderness is a model of a journey of faith, in that we may experience "both a lack of trust in God's promise and a reaffirmation of a commitment to that promise."

Ask:

- In what ways has this been true in your life?

SCOUTS

Invite volunteers to read these verses about Moses sending scouts to explore the Promised Land:

- Numbers 13:1-3
- Numbers 13:17-20;
- Numbers 13:25-33.

Ask:

- Why did Moses send a leader from each tribe to scout out the Promised Land? (*God commanded that Moses do so.*)
- What characteristics would you expect these tribal leaders to have? (*Remember that the census showed a very large number of people in each tribe.)*
- How did Caleb and Joshua feel about taking possession of the Promised Land? (Numbers 13:30; 14:9).
- How did the other ten leaders feel about taking possession of the Promised Land?
- What reasons do the Jewish sages suggest for the scouts' fear? (*Ideas include: fear of change, new responsibilities, and success.*)
- How might the scouts have anticipated that life would be different in the land of Canaan than it was in the wilderness?
- In the present day, why would a person want to stay on a journey rather than reach the destination? (You may want to offer these examples to start the conversation:
  - ◊ a college student prefers to stay in college rather than graduate;
  - ◊ a couple prolongs an engagement rather than setting a wedding date;

◊ a person remains in a job he or she does not like rather than take steps toward a new career.

- When have you preferred the journey over reaching the destination?

Invite discussion of this statement in the section "Scouts":

- "God intends for us to live in the real world of decisions, action, and moral dilemmas. We must take risks in order to grow."

Optional Activity

As an extension of the "Bible Study and Discussion," offer time for participants to share responses to this question for each group member:

- In what ways does (name of participant) share God's blessings and reflect God's presence and love?

You may do this as a group discussion or anonymously. If anonymously, give each participant enough three-by-five cards so they have one for each person in the group. Instruct participants to (1) write one group member's name on each card so they have a card for each person in the group; (2) write a response to the question above for each person. When everyone has finished writing, collect the cards and read the responses. At the end of the activity give each participant the cards with the responses written about her or him.

Wrapping Up

Closing Activity

Highlight this statement from the section "Scouts": "We are called to create a space for God among the challenges of life, not in the isolated wilderness where manna falls from heaven, and everything is taken care of."

Read Numbers 15:37-41. Ask:

- What reminds you of God's presence and God's call in your life?
- How do you create a space for God in the midst of the challenges of life?

CLOSING PRAYER

Loving God, thank you for the Torah. Guide us as we study these ancient writings. Help us to listen carefully so that we may hear what you are saying to us today through these holy words. Amen.

Session 6

Deuteronomy

Planning the Session

SESSION GOALS

- Affirm the Torah as a source of truth, wisdom, and transformation.
- Explore what Deuteronomy 6:5 teaches us about what it means to love God.
- Embrace gratitude and memory as vital aspects of our relationship with God.

BIBLICAL FOUNDATION

- Deuteronomy 1:1; 6:5; 8:17-18; 26:4-10

BEFORE THE SESSION

- Set up a table in the room with nametags and markers, Bibles, and extra copies of *Reading the Old Testament Through Jewish Eyes* if these are still needed;
- For the "Leading into the Study" discussion, write the heading "Words" on a markerboard or large sheet of paper.
- For the study and discussion of Deuteronomy 6:5, write the three questions on separate pieces of paper to distribute to the small groups.

- *The "Bible Study and Discussion" and "Book Study and Discussion" are combined in this session's plan.

GETTING STARTED

GREETINGS AND INTRODUCTIONS

- Greet participants as they arrive.
- If there are newcomers allow time for introductions.
- Review information from Housekeeping in session 1 including the importance of confidentiality within the group.

LEADING INTO THE STUDY

Call attention to the markerboard or sheet of paper with the heading, "Words."

Instruct participants to call out responses to the following question. Recruit a volunteer to write responses on the board or paper and another volunteer to set a timer for one minute. Ask:

- What comes to mind when you hear the word, *Words*?

After the minute is up invite the group to comment about the responses.

Read these Scripture verses and explanations:

- Genesis 1:3: God used words and spoke creation into being.
- Genesis 1:26: Note this quote from *Reading the Old Testament Through Jewish Eyes*: "Human beings are created in the image of God because, like God, we create through words."
- Genesis 2:7: Call attention to these two translations, which Rabbi Moffic pointed out: "man became a living being" and "man became a *speaking* being."

Remind the group that one of our goals for this study is to grow in our understanding of the Torah as a source of "truth, wisdom, and transformation."

OPENING PRAYER

Loving God and Holy God, thank you for speaking the world into being and for creating us in your image. Thank you for the words in the Torah that reveal your love for us and invite us to live in relationship with you. Let us speak words that reveal our love and gratitude for you and that draw others to have faith in you; in the name of your Son Jesus Christ, we pray. Amen.

VIDEO STUDY AND DISCUSSION

Invite participants to consider these questions as they view the video:

- When you think about your legacy, what parts of your faith seem most important to pass on to the next generation? Why?
- Rabbi Moffic says that we never fully realize all of our dreams. How do you respond to this notion? What do you think it says about the nature of life, of faith, and of our relationship with God?
- Rabbi Moffic says that the Torah speaks to our hearts. Do you experience your faith primarily as a matter of the heart? Why or why not?
- What is one thing you've learned in this study that has shaped your faith in God? How have your eyes been opened to the Torah in a new way?

Following the video, invite volunteers to share their responses to the questions above.

Bible and Book Study and Discussion

DEUTERONOMY 1:1

Share background information about the Book of Deuteronomy:

- Its Hebrew name is *Devarim*, which means "words."
- The book includes four speeches that are Moses's last words to the people of Israel.
- The setting is "On the other side of the Jordan, in the land of Moab" (Deuteronomy 1:5) before the people cross over into the land of Canaan.

Read Deuteronomy 1:1, printed in *Reading the Old Testament Through Jewish Eyes*. Ask:

- How is the Moses who speaks to Israel at the end of the forty-year wilderness journey different from the Moses who met God at the burning bush? (*He is a confident speaker now.*)

Read Deuteronomy 1:3 printed below:

> *It was in the fortieth year, on the first day of the eleventh month, that Moses addressed the Israelites in accordance with the instructions that the* Lord *had given him for them.*

Emphasize that God prepares the Israelites for new life in the land of Canaan with *words* spoken through Moses. Ask:

- In what ways have words *prepared* you for a new life?
- How have words *created* a new reality for you? (*for example, wedding vows*)

DEUTERONOMY 6:5

Read Deuteronomy 6:4-5:

Hear, O Israel! The LORD *is our God, the* LORD *alone. You shall love the* LORD *your God with all your heart and with all your soul and with all your might.*

Share these key points:

- This is the Jewish prayer, the Shema.
- Jesus quoted the Shema in Mark 12:28-31.
- Deuteronomy 6:5 is the most important commandment and encompasses several dimensions of love.

Create three small groups and assign these questions:

- Group 1—What does it mean to love the Lord your God with all your heart?
- Group 2—What does it mean to love the Lord your God with all your soul?
- Group 3—What does it mean to love the Lord your God with all your might?

Offer these instructions to the small groups:

- Refer to the section "Love the LORD Your God" as you consider your assigned question.
- Be prepared to report your findings to the whole group.
- Let the groups know how much time is available for them to work.
- Offer each group paper and markers to make notes for their report.

If you have fewer than six participants in your class, research all three questions together as a group. If you have a large number of participants, create six small groups and assign each question to two groups.

After the allotted time call the groups back together and let each group share its findings. Then ask:

- What have you learned about this commandment that you did not know before?
- What new insights have you gained about what it means to love God?
- What aspects of loving God are the most challenging for you, and why?

DEUTERONOMY 8:16-18

Introduce this Scripture by asking:

- What did God provide for the Israelites during the wilderness journey?

Then read aloud Deuteronomy 6:10-12, explaining that it is a description of what God will provide for the Israelites in the land of Canaan.

Next, read Deuteronomy 8:17-18.

Note that the Israelites will have access to two types of wealth in the land of Canaan:

- inherited wealth;
- wealth they acquire by using their abilities to work.

Ask:

- How might inherited wealth draw a person away from God?
- How might wealth acquired through work draw a person away from God? (*Note Rabbi Moffic's observations about "entitlement" during the discussion of these questions.*)

- Why are Moses's words of warning in Deuteronomy 8:17-18 important for the Israelites as they prepare to enter the Promised Land of Canaan?

Invite discussion of these two quotes from Rabbi Moffic:

> "Gratitude will prevent the Israelites from forgetting the source of their abundance."

> "the idea of gratitude…makes little sense without God"

Ask:

- What helps you nurture an attitude of thanksgiving to God?

Close this discussion by saying or singing the Doxology together. It begins "Praise God, from whom all blessings flow" (#95 *UM Hymnal* or https://hymnary.org/text/praise_god_from_whom_all_blessings_ken).

DEUTERONOMY 26:4-10

Invite a volunteer to read Deuteronomy 26:4-10. Ask:

- Why is this Scripture important?
- In what ways do you give your first fruits to God?
- Why is the practice of giving first fruits to God an act of faith and courage? (*It requires that we live with uncertainty.*)

Invite discussion of this quote from Rabbi Moffic:

> "History is what we learn at a high school or university. Memory is what we cherish in our homes and houses of worship."

Ask:

- What memories do you cherish, especially as these relate to your spiritual life and growth?

Optional Activity

Read Genesis 12:1-3, and then read the last paragraph of chapter 6. Ask:

- How are Jews and Christians participants in the same story?
- What discoveries have you made during this study that help you understand the Old Testament as "the bridge" that connects Jews and Christians to God and to each other?

Wrapping Up

CLOSING ACTIVITY

Remind the group that one of the goals for this study is to affirm the Torah as a source of "truth, wisdom, and transformation." Ask:

- How have you grown in your understanding of the Torah as a source of "truth, wisdom, and transformation"?
- What new insights has God given you during this study?
- How have you grown in faith?

CLOSING PRAYER

(Since this is the last session you may want to offer your own prayer in place of or in addition to the closing prayer printed below.)

Loving God, thank you for the Torah. Guide us as we continue to study these ancient writings. Help us to listen carefully so that we may hear what you are saying to us today through these holy words. Amen.

www.ingramcontent.com/pod-product-compliance
Lightning Source LLC
LaVergne TN
LVHW031134050526
838084LV00016B/71

9781791006266